A GIFT FOR: _____

FROM: _____

DATE: _____

Life Principles for the Graduate

Nine truths for living God's way

CHARLES F. STANLEY

Thomas Nelson
Since 1798

ISBN: 978-1-4002-5333-3

24 25 26 27 28 29 MAN 6 5 4 3 2 1

Printed in India

Contents

A Lifelong Process
of Becoming

As you approach graduation, you probably are thinking more than ever about your future. The decisions you are making will affect all that lies ahead, and you're trying to create the best life possible for yourself. Throughout my many years, I have come to understand one thing clearly: Only God can help you live a truly extraordinary life.

When you place your hope in temporal things—money, social status, achievements, acceptance, or even the love of family and friends—your foundation will inevitably crumble. Worldly comforts are no defense against the tumultuous storms that life often delivers. If you are to stand strong, your identity must be based on something greater than what the world offers.

For believers, life is not about who you are but Whose you are. Understanding this is extremely important because it impacts your personal relationship with God as well as your future. Your goal is to get to know Him and, in the process, get yourself out of the way so He can move in and through you. He has a distinct purpose for your life, and He wants you to understand it. When you finally see how beloved you are and how great your calling is, you will sense a desire growing within you to live for Him and in His power.

The Bible offers numerous principles for walking successfully with the Lord. It also teaches us how to live a strong, passionate, and committed life as we grow in faith. In this book, I will address nine time-tested ways God reveals His plans and purposes for our lives. They are based on His principles and offer the right pattern for success, hope, peace, and victory.

Becoming the masterpiece God created you to be is a lifelong process in which He is continually shaping you into a unique reflection of His Son. It is my prayer that you will embrace the process fully and, in so doing, discover the extraordinary life God has planned for you.

Charles F. Stanley

`

chapter one

Surrender:
The Starting Point

Surrender Is the First Step

"For if the willingness is present, it is acceptable according to what a person has, not according to what he does not have."
–2 Corinthians 8:12

God designed your life for His glory. Even before you knew Him, He knew you intimately: "LORD, You have searched me and known me. You know when I sit down and when I get up; You understand my thought from far away. You scrutinize my path and my lying down, and are acquainted with all my ways" (Psalm 139:1-3). When we surrender ourselves to God, we exchange our old thoughts, feelings, and desires for new ones. By faith, we believe that God is who He says He is and that He will do exactly what He has promised.

Each one of us has been blessed with talents to be used for God's glory and work. Yielding to Him is the first step in the process of discovering those gifts and the wondrous purpose for your life.

We still can reach our goals, overcome our failures, and enjoy success, but for a different reason. Instead of boasting about what we have achieved on our own, we can enjoy what God has given abundantly. Our lives become reflections of His life and love rather than a checklist of human accomplishments.

Submit yourself to God. Fulfillment comes only when you decide to love God and give Him all of you. This does not mean that you settle for second best or stop doing what you have been gifted to do. Instead, you come to a point where you ask God to use you to the fullest so that others will come to know Him and experience His forgiveness and unconditional love. Those who have never discovered the wondrous joy that comes from loving and serving God have yet to experience His eternal fulfillment.

God has a plan for your life—a life that is exceptional: "'For I know the plans that I have for you,' declares the LORD, 'plans for prosperity and not for disaster, to give you a future and a hope'" (Jeremiah 29:11). When you trust and seek God, He will teach you how to live above your circumstances. Each one of us has been blessed with talents to be used for God's glory and work. Yielding to Him is the first step in the process of discovering those gifts and the marvelous purpose for your life.

We Can Rely on God's Great Love

"We have come to know and have believed the love which God has for us. God is love, and the one who remains in love remains in God,

and God remains in him … There is no fear in love, but perfect love drives out fear, because fear involves punishment, and the one who fears is not perfected in love." –1 John 4:16, 18

So often we run from God, thinking we need to escape His punishment or avoid doing some task He wants us to do. But what we are actually doing is missing His best for us.

God is omniscient. He knows all about us. He knows what we've done in the past and what we will do in the future. The awesome thing about His love is that it never stops. He loves us the same today as He did yesterday, and His love for us will never change. When we feel as though we have failed in life, He comes to us and raises up a banner of hope on our behalf: "Hope

We must accept and apply a crucial truth to our hearts: It is God's unconditional love that changes us and brings lasting fulfillment.

does not disappoint, because the love of God has been poured out within our hearts through the Holy Spirit who was given to us" (Romans 5:5).

Why is it so difficult to live the Christian life? And why do so many believers end up distressed and unsatisfied? The answers to these questions are found in our ability to accept and apply a crucial truth to our hearts: It is God's unconditional love that changes us and brings lasting fulfillment. Once we understand and accept that there is no greater love than the love of God, we will be ready to take the first step toward living the life He has planned for us.

What goals do you hope to achieve? What dreams has God placed within your heart? Despite your fears and insecurities, you can achieve the goals He has given. There is a way to live each day satisfied and blessed.

God created you in the image of His Son, the Lord Jesus Christ, and His power exists within you. Surrendering to His will and purpose is one of the first steps in achieving a life of fulfillment. Once you begin your journey into His blessings, you will never want to turn back. The world may promise fame and fortune, but in terms of true contentment, it does not deliver. There is a cost involved whenever you go against God's best. Instead of falling prey to sin and failure, decide to stand firm in your faith by trusting Him to guide you in a direction that will lead to unimaginable blessings.

Abiding in Christ

"For this reason I have allowed you to remain, in order to show you My power and ... proclaim My name throughout the earth." –Exodus 9:16

Years ago, I faced a difficult time. I was working tirelessly to please God. Finally, I came to a point of burnout. More than likely, someone reading this book is facing the same thing. You want to keep your grades up, so you work overtime to achieve your goals. Even when you could take time off from studying, you burn the midnight oil. Or perhaps you just can't bring yourself to open a single textbook for more than a few minutes. You know you need to study, but your mind keeps drifting.

> *By abiding, we discover that God sharpens our talents, purifies our minds, and prepares us for service in His kingdom.*

God ministered to me through John 15: "Remain in Me, and I in you. Just as the branch cannot bear fruit of itself but must remain in the vine, so neither can you unless you remain in Me. I am the vine, you are the branches; the one who remains in Me, and I in him bears much fruit, for apart from Me you can do nothing" (vv. 4–5).

The person who abides in the Lord lives not for him- or herself but for Jesus Christ. I discovered that it was not my responsibility to strive for anything. My part was to submit my life to God and allow Him to live His life through me. With that discovery, an enormous weight was removed from my life. Peace unlike anything I'd ever known filled my heart. The energy and strength of Jesus became mine.

By abiding, we discover that God takes our thoughts and conforms them to His will and purpose. He sharpens our talents, purifies our minds, and prepares us for service in His kingdom.

Our treasures—the things we hold dear—become offerings of praise and worship to Him. We begin doing what He has called us to do, at the right time and in the right way. Learning how to plan with His goals in mind is crucial to every area of life. He wants to refocus our spiritual eyesight so we see only Him and not the things that make us feel fearful or unsure. We don't have to waste valuable time, and we don't have to work compulsively to do our best. He has set the right pace for our journey. We can rest because He is in control of all things and because we know that He has a plan and purpose for our existence.

Your Personal Mission

"Delight yourself also in the LORD, and He shall give you the desires of your heart. Commit your way to the LORD, trust also in Him, and He shall bring it to pass." —Psalm 37:4-5 NKJV

I often encouraged those in my congregation to write a mission statement for their lives, and you should do the same. Ask God to show you how He wants you to live. You are never too young or too old to set goals with His mission in mind. Each person who dedicates his or her life to God is given a valuable role to play in His kingdom.

We may not realize the impact of our lives on others. However, God does. He is looking for people who are willing to serve Him. When we say yes to His plans, He will take care of all the details.

Ask Him, "Lord, how do You want me to invest my life?" It may involve something other than your vocation—a job may or may not represent God's purpose for you. We are called to be Christ's disciples in every area of life. Peter, Andrew, and John spent three to four years with the Savior. During that time, Jesus laid a basic foundation for their futures.

Success God's way includes doing what He has given you to do. It is a matter of simple, basic trust in God.

The same can be true for you. Whether you know it or not, God is personally involved in your life. He loves you with an everlasting love, and He wants to demonstrate it to you—so draw near to Him. No matter what has happened in the past, He has plans that stretch far beyond this moment in time.

One of the foundations of the Christian life is the act of spending time with Christ. When our lives and hearts are focused on Him, we will discover His personalized purpose and will for us.

Often people ask the question, *What does God want me to do?* This seems easy to answer, especially when there is a plan to follow—a well-charted major or a career path after graduation. However, His Word says, "Trust in the LORD with all your heart and do not lean on your own understanding. In all your ways acknowledge Him, and He will make your paths straight" (Proverbs 3:5-6). Success God's way includes doing what He has given you to do. It is a matter of simple, basic trust in Him.

Peace and a sense of satisfaction are gifts to those who let go of personal desires and experience the reality of God's goodness. Learning to abide instead of striving teaches you to place your trust in Someone who knows much more than you do about what is to come. Once you have experienced God's goodness, you'll never want to return to a life of straining for outcomes. You will want to know more about your Savior and how your life can better reflect His love and grace to others.

God's Workmanship

"For we are His workmanship, created in Christ Jesus for good works,

**which God prepared beforehand so that we would walk in them."
–Ephesians 2:10**

Understanding your position in Christ is the rudder that directs everything you do. Believing the truth about who God says you are—a genuine masterpiece—is essential to your future. You are the creation of God's hands, and He wants you to be a reflection of His glory and character: "We all, with unveiled faces, looking as in a mirror at the glory of the Lord, are being transformed into the same image from glory to glory, just as from the Lord, the Spirit" (2 Corinthians 3:18).

> *You are the creation of God's hands, and He wants you to be a reflection of His glory and character.*

He wants you to understand the reason you were created (and then re-created through Christ) as well as what your purpose in life is. When you do, you will be energized to live for God through His power.

God wants us to experience joy in Him. We were created for excellence, and from His perspective, our lives represent infinite possibilities. Trusting Him and understanding His great love for us opens the door to a rich, satisfying life.

chapter two

Grace:
Why We Need It

We Are Lost Without Christ

"But when the kindness of God our Savior and His love for mankind appeared, He saved us, not on the basis of deeds which we did in righteousness, but in accordance with His mercy, by the washing of regeneration and renewing by the Holy Spirit." –Titus 3:4-5

Over the years, I have occasionally heard someone say, "I guess I am just going to hell when I die. There is no way God could love me. I'm beyond His help." Friend, no one is ever beyond God's reach. He loves us, and He created each one of us for His good pleasure. No one should speak so carelessly! It is true that each one of us will spend eternity in

When you receive Christ by faith as your personal Savior, God changes your eternal destiny.

either heaven or hell, but God wants us to know that Jesus Christ–His only begotten Son–came to die on a cross to pay the sin debt of all humanity and thereby reconcile us to the Father. And our unconditionally loving God has made it possible for anyone to trust in Jesus as Savior and Lord. When you receive Christ by faith as your personal Savior, God changes your eternal destiny. One moment lost, the next moment saved. Formerly headed for hell, now with a home in heaven.

Without God's grace, we would be utterly without hope. But amazingly, He offers us eternal life in Christ. The best and most important thing we can do is accept this free gift of an unshakable foundation and the promise of a glorious future.

For you—a student with a bright future, this truth is very important. It means once you accept Christ as your Savior, you are no longer alone. You can turn to Him and ask for His help when you are studying for a final, as well as when you are preparing your course schedule for the next term. He is walking with you every step of the way. He knows when you are low in confidence, lack funds, or have grades that ended up not meeting your expectations. He wants you to know that you are not a failure. You are His, and He is committed to you and your future.

Our Great Savior

"Jesus ... because He continues forever, holds His priesthood permanently. Therefore He is also able to save forever those who come to God through Him, since He always lives to make intercession for them." –Hebrews 7:24-25

Some people ask why we celebrate the resurrection. The main reason is that Jesus, our Lord and Savior, is alive; only Christ arose from the dead. No other religious founder can say this. It is very important for you to understand the resurrection because the same power—His resurrection power—is living in you today through the presence of the Holy Spirit.

We celebrate an empty tomb because the One we love, follow, and serve is no longer there. Now, if the Savior arose from the dead, where is He? Scripture tells us that He is seated at the right hand of God, interceding on your behalf. That is, as you pray, He prays for you, telling the Father your needs, your heartaches, and your deepest desires (Hebrews 7:25). Moreover, Jesus is preparing a place for you and me to be with Him in heaven (John 14:2-3). In the meantime, He is arranging all the events necessary for your future and for His return.

His resurrection has given us a very definite purpose for being alive. He has saved us so that we would reflect His life in our work, our ways, our words, and our walk.

First John 2:1-2 reminds us that the Lord is our Advocate. You see, when the Son of God saved us, He knew we would not live perfect lives. He knew we would sin against Him, so He intercedes for us. This defense is based not merely upon our confession and repentance for the forgiveness of sin, but upon the fact that He laid down His life and paid our sin debt in full. When Jesus went to the cross, He died a substitutionary, sacrificial death on our behalf, so we can be absolutely confident that our sins are totally forgiven. Salvation has nothing to do with our behavior, but it has everything to do with the grace, love, goodness, and mercy of God and the blood of Jesus Christ.

His resurrection has given us a very definite purpose for being alive. He has saved us so that we would reflect His life in our work, our ways, our words, and our walk. That is why you and I are the body of Christ. He is looking through our eyes, hearing through our ears, speaking through our voices, and helping through our hands. Having created us for Himself, He desires that you and I walk in holiness and righteousness before Him. We are to be Christ's representatives, pointing people to Him and reflecting His light to a world in desperate need.

God's Love Frees Us From Bondage

"It was for freedom that Christ set us free; therefore keep standing firm and do not be subject again to a yoke of slavery." –Galatians 5:1

Accepting the incredibly expansive love of God is not easy. Many people live their lives convinced that they feel distanced from God because of some sin. They pray incessantly for forgiveness, trying to get beyond the grip of sins that, from God's viewpoint, are simply no longer there. It may be hard to believe, but there are strong Christians who live this way, harboring feelings of shame and self-doubt that have more to do with their fear than with reality.

Others know they are saved but have never discovered the true joy and contentment that come from knowing God in a loving and intimate way. One of the primary reasons the apostle Paul wrote to the believers in Colossae was to tell of the awesome freedom that is available to us through Jesus Christ. False teachers

Nothing brings greater joy than knowing that you can obey God and receive His endless blessings.

had entered the fellowship of this New Testament church. They were teaching that while it was right to accept Jesus as the Messiah, one also must live under the regulations of the Mosaic law. Jesus came to set us free from burdens like that. We can obey His law because it has been given to us as a framework for living the abundant life. Nothing brings greater joy than knowing that you can obey God and receive His endless blessings.

However, we cannot attest to God's grace while living in bondage.

Wholeness is found only in Jesus, not in abiding by prescribed rules or regulations. But we always need to remember that our freedom in Christ was very costly. The Father gave His Son so that we can live each day in the light of His freedom and hope. Never abuse this God-given gift by knowingly entering into sin. When He tells you to steer clear of something, He does this for a reason. Most of the time, it is to protect you from harm. Sin destroys, while the love of God brings freedom.

The Christian life is an expression of God's grace rather than a checklist of dos and don'ts. That is what Christianity is all about—freedom to enjoy the life God has given us and freedom to share this truth with others.

An Encounter With Grace

"There are many plans in a man's heart, nevertheless the LORD's counsel—that will stand." –Proverbs 19:21 NKJV

The direction your life takes is affected by many things, such as the environment in which you are living, the decisions you make, and the education you receive. But by far the most powerful influence in a believer's life is the transforming grace of God, which is His kindness toward you regardless of your worthiness.

God's ultimate will is for every believer to be conformed to the likeness of His Son. His grace is responsible for your rebirth, and it directs, moves, and influences you to become increasingly Christlike. In that way, you can say with the apostle Paul, "By the grace of God I am what I am" (1 Corinthians 15:10).

The apostle's life, in fact, is a powerful example of God's transforming grace. In Philippians 3, Paul described how he once depended on his good works, nature, and conduct to gain acceptance before God. He did not originally understand there is only one way to be made acceptable in God's sight—by His grace.

However, encountering the living Christ totally changed Paul, and he explained, "Whatever things were gain to me, these things I have [now] counted as loss because of Christ" (Philippians 3:7). He recognized that all his human titles and achievements had no spiritual value. We, too, must realize we will never merit eternal life by depending on anything we are or anything we do. It is by grace and grace alone that we are saved (Ephesians 2:8-9).

It is out of His gentle love—not condemnation or chastisement—that the heavenly Father arranges the circumstances and challenges of your life.

It was the grace of God that shaped Paul's thinking. He learned that everything he once counted as valuable was actually worthless. What made the difference was the fact that Paul came face-to-face with the Savior on the road to Damascus.

Is God talking to your heart? Is He asking you to do something you don't like or something you are afraid to do? Remember that it is out of His gentle love—not condemnation or chastisement—that the heavenly Father arranges the circumstances and challenges of your life. Whatever He requires of you is always in your best interest and will be part of the process that conforms you to the image of His Son.

Just as it was with the apostle Paul, an encounter with God's grace will change your course—and it will always lead you in the best possible direction. Therefore, don't hesitate to accept His gracious plan. He sees all the potential pitfalls, challenges, and blessings that will come and knows the right way around danger. You can rest in Him.

chapter three

Connecting With God: The Most Effective Way to Live

The Treasure of Knowing Christ

"This is what the LORD says: 'Let no wise man boast of his wisdom, nor let the mighty man boast of his might, nor a rich man boast of his riches; but let the one who boasts boast of this, that he understands and knows Me.'" –Jeremiah 9:23-24

Knowing Jesus as Lord radically rearranges our priorities, alters our perspective, and influences our relationships and decision-making processes. Christ becomes our focus and center. In His presence, we gain indescribable peace.

Knowing Jesus as Lord radically rearranges our priorities, alters our perspective, and influences our relationships.

Prestige, possessions, and power are but "rubbish" when compared with the blessing of knowing Jesus (Philippians 3:8). Discovering His faithfulness, experiencing His help, and embracing His purposes bring significance to every facet of life.

Paul understood that his highest goal was to gain experiential knowledge of Jesus Christ. He was willing to undergo harsh treatment and imprisonment because such things would help him to know the Savior more fully. He was able to tolerate afflictions because he viewed them in the light of a broader spiritual goal:

experiencing the sufficiency of Christ in every situation.

Have you come to the point where you can agree with Paul's confession of dependence on Christ? Do you see the suffering you are facing as a way to know Him in a very personal way? He is close to the brokenhearted. You may be battling temptation and can't believe God would continue to love you. He does. And if you admit your need, He'll give you the strength to conquer every temptation, challenge, and sin.

Is knowing Christ your ultimate goal? If it is, then He will show you how to lay your disappointments and failures at the foot of His cross.

God's promises are sure. When we set our hearts to know Him, He opens our minds to spiritual truth, revealing Himself in wonderful and often unexpected ways. Although the world offers enticing substitutes, nothing can compare to the value of a genuine, growing relationship with Jesus Christ. We read in Colossians 2:3 that "all the treasures of wisdom and knowledge" are hidden in Christ. When our foremost passion is to know God, He assures us He will provide for the rest of our needs (Matthew 6:31-33).

God Wants to Be Known

"The God of our fathers has chosen you that you should know His will, and see the Just One, and hear the voice of His mouth. For you

will be His witness to all men of what you have seen and heard."
—Acts 22:14-15 NKJV

There is quite a difference between knowing something about God and knowing God in a personal, loving way. Far too many people have a superficial knowledge of Him but do not really know the person of Jesus Christ. That can happen only when we cultivate an intimate relationship with Him.

Too many Christians are content knowing that Jesus is their Savior. They are grateful that their sins are forgiven and heaven is their destiny. But they are unwilling to pursue the real meaning of eternal life: knowing Jesus (John 17:3).

For any relationship to grow, we must spend time communicating, listening, and trying to understand more about the other person.

Nothing pleases God more than our full surrender, and He rewards it abundantly. Jesus said, "The one who comes to Me I certainly will not cast out" (John 6:37). But for any relationship to grow, we must spend time communicating, listening, and trying to understand more about the other person.

Do you really want to know God? The way to do that is by knowing Christ: Receive Him as your Savior, who paid your sin debt in full, and

31

then accept His invitation to spend time in private conversation every day. In return, you will receive the incredible opportunity to have a personal, loving relationship with the God of the universe.

You can know His will, His mind, and the reason He works the way He does. He allows disappointment. There will be times that you fail a test—either in the classroom at college or in the classroom of life. When you do, knowing Him makes all the difference. Suddenly, you realize He is on your team and wants only the best for you. Do you know how to trust Him? Do you believe that He has His best for you? It is true. He knows you by name, and He longs to give you His very best—not just for today but for eternity.

Seeking the Lord With All Your Heart

"My sheep listen to My voice, and I know them, and they follow Me."
—John 10:27

To spend time with the Lord and hear His voice, you must be still and quiet. Let's say you're seeking an answer to a pressing need. The most effective way to find the answer is to read God's Word, followed by prayer asking for His wisdom. Then, be quiet and listen for His response. Oftentimes, His answer doesn't come when we're praying but afterward. I think sometimes God delays so that we don't get in the habit of sending up "quick fix-it" prayers. By asking Him and then listening for His response, we may "hear" through circumstances or other revelations.

The more time you spend with the Lord, the more familiar His voice becomes. You'll just know without a doubt that God is speaking to you. How does He make this happen? He speaks to us primarily through His Word. He also will speak through godly, committed believers and the presence of the Holy Spirit, who abides within us.

Some of the greatest lessons I've learned have come through times of extreme difficulty. I can remember asking God to give me guidance for a situation I was facing. Stress was building, and I could not immediately see how He would solve my problems. I believed He would, but it was a matter of walking by faith and trusting Him. Sure enough, as I was praying one day, I sensed Him saying, "Trust Me." That was it. These were the two words that drew me nearer to Him and changed my perspective from one of stress to one of power and strength because I knew His promises do not fail.

He tells us, "Trust in the LORD with all your heart and do not lean on your own understanding. In all your ways acknowledge Him, and He will make your paths straight" (Proverbs 3:5-6). When the bottom to life falls out, you can trust God. He is faithful and true.

As a student, you'll face times when it's unclear what is best. You may find yourself worrying and wondering which way to go. Don't hesitate to ask God to speak to you through His Word. He wants you to come to Him. Then, when you hear His answer, you can know with absolute certainty that God has told you what He's going to do. And He always keeps His word.

We need to spend time in prayer, meditation, and worship. We come not just to receive from Him but to hear from, adore, praise, and delight in Him.

Throughout the years, God has never failed me. He has kept every promise He ever made. Always. There have been times when I wanted to force an answer from Him, but that never works. God has a perfect timetable. He knows exactly when to bring the answer you need. If you ask for something that's not His best, there should be a check in your spirit—something that says, "Beware. That is not God's way." It usually creates a bit of doubt and is an opportunity for you to go to Him in prayer and ask Him to make His will clear.

Over the years, people have said to me, "You mean God cares about this small need or issue in my life?" And I always say, "Absolutely." He may not care if you have hot or cold coffee to drink, but

He cares about every problem, challenge, or dilemma you encounter. And keep in mind that if your petition is not God's best, He will not give you total peace and assurance.

Spiritual intimacy requires quiet moments when He can speak clearly to your heart and you can speak honestly to Him. We need to spend time in prayer, meditation, and worship—coming not just to receive from Him but to hear from, adore, praise, and delight in Him.

We also must give ourselves to the study of Scripture. The Bible reveals who God is and what He has done. If we really want to know Him, we'll set aside time to partake of the living Word and let His divine counsel saturate our minds. Reading spiritual biographies of godly people can also strengthen our walk with God as we observe how He's worked in their lives. They have a great deal to tell us about His ways.

I encourage you to lay aside any desire in your life that supersedes your passion to know Christ. Jesus wants all of you, not just a part. You can begin today to know the Lord on a new, deeper level by admitting your need and asking Him to lead you. When knowing God becomes the passion of your life, you can, like the apostle Paul, learn to "count all things to be loss in view of the surpassing value of knowing Christ Jesus" (Philippians 3:8).

God, Our Father

"You have received a spirit of adoption as sons and daughters by which we cry out, 'Abba! Father!'" —Romans 8:15

When you pray, by what name do you address God? While all the titles we find in Scripture are appropriate, we have the awesome privilege of calling God "Father." I'll never forget the day this reality became clear to me.

I was in my office when our administrative assistant walked in with her 9-month-old daughter. I stood to admire the infant, and before I could offer a single word of praise, she thrust the child into my arms. As I looked down at the tiny baby, I realized she was the same age I was when my father died. Whenever people asked me about him, I would simply say that he died when I was too young to know him. But as I stood holding that little girl, I realized that my father had known *me*. Our relationship with God is the same. He tells us, "Before I formed you in the womb I knew you, and before you were born I consecrated you" (Jeremiah 1:5).

That is the reason Jesus Christ came to earth —to die on the cross for our sins and to make it possible for you and me to know the Father intimately.

The possibility of having a personal relationship with God was a revolutionary concept before Christ lived as a human. The Old Testament contains only about 15 references to God as "Father," and those speak primarily of Him as the Father of the Hebrew people. The idea of Him being a personal God to individuals is not evident until the New Testament. Yet that is the reason Jesus Christ came to earth—to die on the cross for our sins and to make it possible for you and me to know the Father intimately.

The privilege of knowing God as our Father goes beyond familiarity with His matchless grace, love, and kindness and even surpasses knowing Him in His holiness, righteousness, and justice. How wonderful that we—mere creations—are able to know Him personally.

Do you know God as your heavenly Father? If not, realize that He stands ready to adopt you into His family (Romans 8:15; Galatians 3:26). All it takes is a committed desire to know and trust Jesus Christ as your personal Savior.

God Speaks to Us Today

"Call to Me and I will answer you, and I will tell you great and mighty things, which you do not know." —Jeremiah 33:3

The God we serve is not a distant, silent deity. He has been communicating with His creation since the beginning, occasionally in an audible voice, but also in other ways (Exodus 4:4; Hebrews 1:1). Since the first century, He has spoken to us through His Son (Hebrews 1:2), and He continues to speak as we read Scripture, pray, and seek godly counsel from other believers.

You might wonder, *Why would God want to communicate today? What does He have to say to us?* I believe there are several reasons God speaks. The first is that He loves us and desires an intimate bond with His children. As with any growing relationship, conversation must flow in two directions: We must be willing not only to talk to Him but also to listen.

Though we can never fully grasp all the facets of who God is, He wants us to spend our lives discovering more about Him.

A second reason is to give us guidance. God's people today need as much wisdom and counsel as the saints of the Bible did. We still require direction for things like our finances, family, career, church, and health. Divine wisdom is essential if we are to make sound decisions. This is the reason God sent the Holy Spirit to be our Guide and Teacher (John 16:13; 14:26).

Another reason He communicates is to bring us assurance and

comfort. In Scripture, God spoke to numerous people undergoing hardships and persecution, reminding them of His sovereign control over their situations and fortifying their faith. We are no different from the people in biblical times. When you and I go through turbulent experiences in our lives, God wants to strengthen our faith and confidence in Him.

The final—and I believe foremost—reason is that God wants us to know Him. Though we can never fully grasp all the facets of who God is, He wants us to spend our lives discovering more about Him.

What a Friend We Have in Jesus

"You will make known to me the way of life; in Your presence is fullness of joy; in Your right hand there are pleasures forever." –Psalm 16:11

I've known what it's like to feel lonely. Yet I've experienced the most amazing sense of peace, happiness, and joy in my heart because I've never really been alone. There was a time when walking into an empty home bothered me, but after a while the Lord reminded me that He is constantly present. He changed a complaint into a real comfort because I came to understand that He is adequate and would turn the lonely hours into a fruitful time in my life. In fact, He's always done that.

There is no substitute for personal intimacy with God. Nothing compares to it—it's the key to everything. Most people are looking for an exciting and fulfilling life, and they're looking in all the wrong places: money, prestige, and relationships. They are looking for something that they can achieve to bring about fulfillment or for someone they can meet who will make their life more meaningful. But there isn't anything we can do or anyone we can meet who will sufficiently fill the void in our hearts. As Blaise Pascal said, the "infinite abyss" in us "can be filled only with an infinite and immutable object; in other words by God himself." Only the gift of His Spirit abiding in us is totally adequate for our needs.

To experience intimacy with the heavenly Father, you must genuinely regard Him as more important than everything else you pursue in life.

To experience intimacy with the heavenly Father, you must genuinely regard Him as more important than everything else you pursue in life. It is important to have goals and relationships, but your primary ambition should be to know God. When I think about all the things I have been through in my life, I consider my relationship with God absolutely paramount. He has always been there to assure me and bring me through life's trials, no matter how hard they have been.

chapter four

Trusting the Lord: His Purpose Will Move Heaven and Earth

God Is Trustworthy

"Faithful is He who calls you, and He also will do it."

–1 Thessalonians 5:24

Do you trust God with your life? He created you and knows you completely. He understands your weaknesses and your desire to love Him. Even when you feel as though you've failed Him, He is quick to forgive and remind you of His love.

Because they thought Jesus had died on the cross, several disciples returned to their former occupation. Instead of living by faith and doing what God had called them to do, they went back out on the Sea of Galilee to fish (John 21:3-4)! However, before the crucifixion, Jesus had said that He would return to them, and He fulfilled that promise. In fact, God has kept every promise He ever made. This is why we can trust Him with every aspect of our lives.

God has kept every promise He has ever made. This is why we can trust Him with every aspect of our lives.

Have you ever wondered how God views our lack of faith? It is certain that He will never condemn us (Romans 8:1). We know this because, although Peter denied knowing Christ, Jesus welcomed him back. We may falter and fail, but God does not want us to focus on our shortcomings. Instead, He wants us to set our focus on Him. God evaluates our lives not according to our ability to remain faithful but according to His faithfulness and the work that was accomplished at Calvary. While He does not want us to yield to temptation, He knows there will be times when we fall. But no matter what, we always remain the beneficiaries of His endless grace and eternal love.

Our Lives Are in His Hands

"The plan of the LORD stands forever, the plans of His heart from generation to generation ... Our heart rejoices in Him, because we trust in His holy name." –Psalm 33:11, 21

God is perfect in His love, infinite in His wisdom, and sovereign in His control of the entire universe.

Our lives belong to our sovereign, all-knowing, loving God, and nothing can touch us except what He allows. Sometimes that includes hardship and suffering, which leaves us wondering, *How can this possibly be good?* And yet many people who have gone through tremendous trials later look back and say, "I hated the difficulty while I was going through it, but now, looking back, I can see why He allowed it." Not everyone fully attains such spiritual insight. Yet it happens frequently enough that we can take comfort, realizing God has His purposes and, with perfect timing, will bring blessing from our trials (Romans 8:28).

When you face struggles, remind yourself that God has your best interests in mind. He wants you to trust Him and surrender your life to Him. There is no reason to doubt, because He is perfect in love, infinite in wisdom, and sovereign over the entire universe. Why should believers ever fret when, even in the deepest, darkest valleys, there can be abiding joy and confidence? No matter what happens, our all-loving, all-wise, all-powerful heavenly Father has you in the palm of His hand.

Walking in Christ

"If we live by the Spirit, let's follow the Spirit as well." —Galatians 5:25
Scripture frequently uses the image of walking as a description of the Christian life. For example, we are told to walk as children of light, to walk in the truth, to walk according to the Spirit, and to walk in love. Colossians 2:6 uses this expression to give us an important command: "As you have received Christ Jesus the Lord, so walk in Him." The question we must ask is, What does it mean to walk in Christ?

Here the word *in* does not have a literal usage the way it does in a sentence such as "The hammer is in the toolbox." Rather, it refers to a vital relationship—a union between the believer and the Lord. What God desires is not simply to forgive sins, but to develop a close, ever-deepening personal relationship with each of His children. He wants us to realize that the Son of God is the source of everything.

In other words, Jesus Christ is to the believer what blood is to the body: indispensable to life.

> *Just as it is impossible to walk while standing still, believers are either moving forward in their Christian life or going backward.*

Therefore, "walking in Christ" refers to a dynamic relationship with the Lord. Just as it is impossible to walk while standing still, believers are either moving forward in their Christian life or going backward. The key for making progress is found in that same verse from Colossians: "As you have received Christ Jesus the Lord, so walk in Him." How did you and I receive Christ? By faith. To be born again, we trusted the testimony of God's Word. The Christian life is to be "walked"—or lived out—the same way.

Followers of Jesus Christ are commanded to "walk by faith, not by sight" (2 Corinthians 5:7). We must take the first step by faith, and then another step by trusting that our omniscient, loving God has our best interests in mind. Walking in faith means having a personal relationship with Jesus Christ—a relationship that results in trusting Him for every circumstance and believing He will do what is right and what benefits us every time, without exception.

The Way of Faith

"And we know that God causes all things to work together for good to those who love God, to those who are called according to His purpose." –Romans 8:28

What do you do when facing a seemingly insurmountable challenge? Proverbs 3:5-6 gives this instruction: "Trust in the LORD with all your heart and do not lean on your own understanding. In all your ways acknowledge Him, and He will make your paths straight."

God has a purpose for every situation we encounter. There are no coincidences with Him. He is the architect behind every blessing that comes our way. And in times of trial and sorrow, He is working to bring goodness and hope out of each difficulty.

God has a purpose for every situation we encounter. There are no coincidences with Him.

When God gave the command to sacrifice Isaac on the altar, Abraham didn't cower in fear or agonize over how the Lord would provide for him. He trusted God, and in doing so, he was able to have fellowship with Him. Earlier, Scripture had said Abraham believed God and his belief was "credited" to him as "righteousness" (Genesis 15:6).

There are two things that are essential to living a faith-motivated life. First, we must believe that God exists. Second, we must believe that He will do what He has promised to do. Hebrews 11:6 tells us that "without faith it is impossible to please [God], for the one who comes to God must believe that He exists, and that He proves to be One who rewards those who seek Him." Faith is not a goal that we must work to achieve. It is the overflow of a personal relationship with God, as natural as breathing.

Making Our Faith Strong

"My salvation and my glory rest on God; the rock of my strength, my refuge is in God. Trust in Him at all times, you people; pour out your hearts before Him; God is a refuge for us." –Psalm 62:7-8

God has a plan to develop our faith. He takes our limited trust and transforms it into something strong and mighty that can conquer anything. This is often why He allows us to face adversity and challenges of all kinds. In times of extreme pressure, God stretches our faith and deepens our dependence on Him. Without strong, abiding trust, we will quickly yield to temptation and fear, especially when the difficulty is intense.

The Lord grew David's trust until it was unshakable, and He wants to do this for us too. Whether we're starting a new chapter of life or ending an old one, God wants to teach us to trust Him every moment.

God wants to teach us to trust Him every moment.

Discouragement is one of Satan's primary methods of attack. Once we have accepted Christ as our Savior, the Enemy goes to work on our emotions by trying to make us believe that God doesn't really love us and that we aren't worthy of His love. Satan wants us to feel defeated and discouraged, because if he can make us give up, then we will abandon our commitment to God.

Troubles may come in the form of financial loss, the death of a loved one, a serious illness, a broken relationship, or the betrayal of a friend. But God does not want us to sink into feelings of doubt and worry. He loves us with an "everlasting love," and He is our ever-present help, our rock, our fortress, our deliverer, our refuge, our strength, and our infinite stronghold (Jeremiah 31:3; Psalm 18).

chapter five

Obedience:
It Always
Brings Blessing

God Values Obedience

"The LORD leads with unfailing love and faithfulness all who keep his covenant and obey his demands." —Psalm 25:10 NLT

One of the most important principles a Christian can learn is obedience. When we obey God, we will experience His blessing; when we don't, we will miss out.

The more familiar we become with God's Word, the more we will understand the importance of submission. God's laws are not designed to deprive us of pleasure or prosperity. Rather, they are intended to protect us from hurting ourselves and others and to guide us toward the fulfillment He wants us to experience.

God's laws are not designed to deprive us of pleasure or prosperity. Rather, they are intended to protect us from hurting ourselves and others and to guide us toward the fulfillment He wants us to experience.

When pressured, we may be tempted to compromise and dismiss Scripture's teachings in favor of self-reliance or worldly solutions. Sometimes we will have to make choices that result in rejection, loss, confrontation, or hardship. But however difficult our circumstances become, we can respond to them with confidence in the One who empowers us to do His will. Has God ever made a mistake, been too late, or proven Himself inadequate? No! Our heavenly Father is all-powerful and consistently faithful.

The Bible teaches us that we reap what we sow. When we obey God, we always get His best. When we don't, life will become much harder than it needs to be. For us as Christians, making a commitment to obey God is essential to our faith because obedience and faith are inseparable. We demonstrate our trust in God by complying with His will. And every time we do, we will reap the rewards He has designed for us.

The Key to God's Heart

"Then Jesus said to His disciples, 'If anyone wants to come after Me, he must deny himself, take up his cross, and follow Me. For whoever wants to save his life will lose it; but whoever loses his life for My sake will find it.'" –Matthew 16:24-25

I still remember the key that unlocked the door to our house. I was in the first grade, and I would hide it under a rock as I left each morning. When I came home in the afternoon, a wonderful sense of relief flooded over me when I lifted the stone and saw it was still there. The key was important because it allowed me to enter the place where we lived—where my needs were met and I felt my mother's love and care.

More than likely, you have a set of keys—to your house, car, dorm room, or some other important entryway. But do you have the key to someone's heart? When you have that, you know how to access what is inside. You know how to speak directly to that person and understand how he or she feels.

The key to God's heart is obedience, but too many people don't realize this. We're taught to be independent, and the idea of obedience doesn't always go over well. However, God does not fashion Himself according to our preferences. Obedience is what He requires—and it cannot be half-hearted or insincere.

When you do the right thing from God's perspective, He is going to bless you.

Is obeying always the right choice? Absolutely and with no exceptions. Jesus said, "Anyone who loves me will obey my teaching. My Father will love them, and we will come to them and make our home with them" (John 14:23 NIV). There is an important thing to remember about obedience: It always leads to blessing. No matter what is required, when you do the right thing from God's perspective, He is going to bless you. Instead of feeling a sense of dread and anxiety, you will have a sense of confidence and peace. You can do many things to honor God, but the one thing that He prizes above all others is your willingness to obey.

Obedience Can Turn Everything Around

"For this is what the Lord GOD, the Holy One of Israel, has said: 'In repentance and rest you will be saved, in quietness and trust is your strength.'" –Isaiah 30:15

God's simple requests are often stepping stones to life's greatest blessings. Simon Peter gives us an illustration of what happens when we say yes to God. In Luke 5:1-11, people were pressing in around Jesus while He was preaching. The Lord wanted to use Peter's boat as a floating platform from which to address the throng, so He asked the future apostle to push the vessel out a little way (v. 3). This request was not particularly remarkable, but Peter's obedience was. His willingness to do what the Savior asked paved the way for multiple blessings on that day. From his example,

We must recognize that obeying God is always the wise course of action. Jesus turned an empty boat into a full one. He can also take our emptiness and change it into something splendid and thriving.

we learn just how important it is to obey the Lord, no matter what His request may be.

Immediately, the people were blessed by Peter's obedience because they could hear Jesus' words as He taught. Then, when the lesson was completed, the Lord said to Peter, "Put out into the deep water and let down your nets for a catch" (v. 4). Here was another opportunity for Peter to obey or say no. He had worked the entire night with the hopes of catching fish. But he had returned empty-handed and exhausted. Now, Jesus was telling him to head back out onto the Sea of Galilee at a time of day when no one would even bother trying. But notice what Peter did and how he responded. He obeyed the Savior, and because of his obedience, two overflowing boatloads of fish were pulled to shore (vv. 6-7). Saying yes resulted in a miracle that absolutely transformed Peter's life and the lives of those around him.

Like Peter, we must recognize that obeying God is always the wise course of action. Jesus turned an empty boat into a full one. He can also take our emptiness and change it into something splendid and thriving.

Obedience—Always

"We are destroying arguments and all arrogance raised against the knowledge of God, and we are taking every thought captive to

the obedience of Christ." –2 Corinthians 10:5

Obedience can be a challenge, especially if we think we know more about our lives and circumstances than God does. However, the inescapable truth is this: Obedience is essential to pleasing Him—not just in times of deep, serious temptation but also in moments of simpler testing.

Can you remember the last time you were tempted to do the opposite of what you knew the Lord desired? Deep inside, you probably understood what was right, but a struggle ensued in your mind. You probably asked yourself something like, *Should I obey God or disobey Him and hope that He won't notice?* In truth, nothing good can come from disobeying God, and in the long run, nothing bad can come from obeying Him. When we decide to obey God, we choose wisdom, which is the way to blessing.

God's concern for us springs from His deep love and devotion. He requires our obedience because He knows the devastating effect that disobedience and sin will have on our lives.

Disobedience tells the Lord we believe we know better than He does. However, our self-assurance evaporates when it comes face-to-face with the sovereignty of almighty God. That's why, when standing in God's presence, the prophet Isaiah cried out, "Woe to me ... I am a man of unclean lips, and I live among a people of unclean lips" (Isaiah 6:5).

God was looking for someone who would take His Word to the people. And Isaiah was His man. He had seen God's glory, and obedience was his only choice. Imagine how different things would have turned out if Isaiah had followed a selfish route rather than the Lord's instructions.

God's concern for us springs from His deep love and devotion. He requires our obedience because He knows the devastating effect that disobedience and sin will have on our lives. God forgives and is willing to restore, but some wrongs have lasting results. Disobedience always leads to disappointment, sorrow, and brokenness. But obedience leads to joy, peace, fulfillment, and security. When you obey the Lord, you will more readily recognize His goodness.

The Blessing of the Holy Spirit

"Work out your own salvation with fear and trembling; for it is God who is at work in you, both to desire and to work for His good pleasure." –Philippians 2:12-13

Many people think they are demonstrating obedience to God by helping others occasionally, avoiding temptation, and attending church. But there is much more to it. True obedience to God means doing what He says, when He says, how He says, as long as He says, until what He asks us to do is accomplished.

Unfortunately, this concept often is rejected in today's culture. We have rationalized disobedience to the point of missing God's best. Do you ever catch yourself wondering why God doesn't answer your prayers? It could have something to do with your level of obedience to Him. If you have accepted Jesus Christ as your Savior and yet are still experiencing great spiritual frustration, there may be a shortcoming in your life that you have not addressed. Perhaps God has asked something of you and, in response, you ignored His words or have done only part of what He required.

Is there one area of your life in which you struggle to be obedient to God's Word? As you read Scripture, does a particular sin come to your attention? If the Lord is bringing something to mind, it could be because at some point, you chose to do things your way instead of His.

Understanding this key distinction between our way and God's way can make a tremendous difference in every believer's life. To avoid disobedience, you must bring your thoughts, actions, words, and goals in line with God's perfect will (2 Corinthians 10:5; Ephesians 5:1). More importantly, when He gives you words of direction, wisdom, or warning, you must heed them completely.

There is good news: Even though we cannot be as perfect and blameless as Christ until the time when we are with Him in heaven, the Holy Spirit enables us to obey Him today. In doing so, we take on the Spirit of Christ. We become like Him in the sense that we want to live holy lives and reflect His love to others.

No matter what He requires of us—whether it be painful or joyful, profitable or costly—God Himself will help us to obey and perform His will.

No amount of human effort can achieve what God gives through His grace. No matter what He requires of us—whether it be painful or joyful, profitable or costly—God Himself will help us to obey and perform His will.

Receiving Jesus Christ as your Savior involves your first act of obedience—praying, "Father, forgive me. I've sinned against You and have been living in rebellion. I'm asking You to forgive me, not because I'm so good, but because I believe Jesus paid my sin debt in full." The moment you do this, the Holy Spirit comes into your heart, and God saves you. He also enables you to walk obediently before Him, in His strength and power.

As I wrote this book, my prayer for all readers—my petition on your behalf—was that you would be obedient to God. That way, you can become the person He wants you to be, do the work He desires, and receive the blessings He has prepared for you.

chapter six

God's Will: It's Worth the Wait

Waiting on the Lord

"Wait for the LORD; be strong and let your heart take courage; yes, wait for the LORD." —Psalm 27:14

When God tells us to wait on His will, He always has a very clear reason, and the reason is, without exception, for our benefit. That's why learning to wait is essential in the Christian life.

Being patient is surely difficult, but failing to wait upon the Lord can bring about disastrous consequences. First, when we do not wait, we get out of line with God's will. Second, we delay His planned blessing for us because we move ahead of His steps. Third, we bring pain and suffering upon others and ourselves. Fourth, we are prone to make snap judgments that quite often turn out to cost us dearly in terms of finances, emotional energy, or relationships.

We live much happier lives when we learn to obey with grace and trust.

Many people are not willing to wait on God for His timing, particularly when it involves the possibility of letting go of something they desire. But when we take our eyes off God and try to manipulate our situation to conform to our will, we usually make a colossal mess of things. Whenever we reach for something that is not of God, it turns to ashes because He will never prosper what we manipulate. No matter how hard we try, it just doesn't work. Either we can repent and wait for the Lord—and likely get everything we need—or we can step ahead of Him and face loss. We live much happier lives when we learn to obey with grace and trust.

Stop and Listen

"Yet those who wait for the LORD will gain new strength; they will mount up with wings like eagles, they will run and not get tired, they will walk and not become weary." —Isaiah 40:31

God is moving and active. He has a definite plan for your life, but He may be calling you to wait awhile. I pray you will discover why for yourself, in His time.

Think of waiting as a determined stillness, during which time you decide not to act until the Lord gives clear direction.

One of the primary reasons believers step out of God's will—and out of fellowship with Him—is that they begin to go forward with their own plans and ignore His wisdom or guidance. They become eager and impatient. Without waiting for clear direction, they move ahead and make decisions without taking time to pray and seek His best. It is important for you to realize what it means to truly wait upon the Lord.

Waiting does not require you to be idle. Instead, it simply means pausing until you receive further instructions. You should think of waiting as a determined stillness, during which time you decide not to act until the Lord gives clear direction.

Yes, it is difficult to stand still when everything in you wants to move. However, wise men and women wait upon the Lord until they have heard from Him. Then, when they finally move, it is with boldness, confidence, courage, strength, and absolute assurance that God will keep His word.

Steadfast Trust

"Some trust in chariots, and some in horses; but we will remember the name of the LORD our God." –Psalm 20:7 NKJV

Waiting patiently for a word from God requires learning how to rest in Him. If you want to hear what He has to say, you must come to the point where you are no longer rushing in body or mind. Clearly, you cannot separate waiting upon the Lord and trusting in Him—these two things go hand in hand.

Patient waiting does not involve looking anxiously around to see what others are doing. How often have you been sure about what the Lord had said but changed your course of action because of what you saw others doing? Or how often have you been tempted to doubt Him because of the negative voices you heard: *Is this the right choice? How do I know that this is Your best, Lord? What if I make a mistake?* God wants to clear up all the clutter. He has a simple, straightforward path, but you must still your heart to discern it.

When it comes to your personal walk with God, the bottom line is this: Are you going to listen to God and do what He says?

Waiting demands patience, and it certainly requires trust. As you wait upon the Lord, you will have to stand strong against the pressure of other people who want to goad you into making a decision that fits their schedules or preferences. Maybe you are in a relationship or a job and don't feel ready to move ahead. If God has not given you the green light, moving forward at the insistence of others is the worst thing you can do.

When it comes to your personal walk with God, the bottom line is this: Are you going to listen to Him and do what He says? Are you going to wait upon Him when your peers become impatient and everything around you is pushing you to move? You can take heart in knowing that God will strengthen you through your waiting. If you trust in Him, He will help you shoulder the weight of your burdens.

When God Seems Far Away

"Therefore we do not lose heart, but though our outer person is decaying, yet our inner person is being renewed day by day. For our momentary, light affliction is producing for us an eternal weight of glory far beyond all comparison, while we look not at the things which are seen, but at the things which are not seen."
–2 Corinthians 4:16-18

For all of us as Christians, there are times when the Lord seems distant and uninterested in our circumstances. We pray and diligently seek His will, but our need, at least from our perspective, remains unmet. We wait and wait but do not hear from Him. In those moments we may ask, *Does God truly have an answer? Does He really care when we hurt and struggle against the pressures of life?*

How should we handle times of spiritual silence when we feel as though He is standing at a distance and won't answer prayers according to our desires and timeline? Take a few moments to read the story of Mary, Martha, and Lazarus in John 11. Each of these people had definite needs.

Lazarus needed a healing touch from God. He was deathly ill (v. 1), and Jesus had the power to heal him. Mary and Martha had tremendous needs as well. How would they survive without Lazarus in a culture where women had very few rights, if any? Jesus knew all this. In fact, the Lord was their close friend and a frequent guest in their home. Once Mary and Martha realized their brother could die, it seemed only right to send for Jesus.

God never leaves us hopeless. He has a plan and a design for our lives that is well fitted for every trial, every sorrow, every heartache, and every problem we face.

As their brother lay dying, Mary and Martha did not understand just how deeply involved God was in their lives. At times, each one of us has failed to understand this. Jesus was determined to demonstrate how much He cared. But first, Mary and Martha would have to wait. And their prayers, though in harmony with God's will, would appear to go unanswered.

Somewhere along the line, Mary and Martha began to understand the sovereignty of God. They had to come to a point where they accepted God's will over their own. Each one of us will face this decision at some time. We may wonder why, on the surface, it appears that God has not met our needs. Yet deep inside, we should understand that God never leaves us hopeless. He has a plan for our lives that is well fitted for every trial, every sorrow, every heartache, and every problem we face.

Never give up! Trust God to the end, and you will see His goodness become a reality in your life.

Determining God's Will in Everything

"For this reason we also, since the day we heard about it, have not ceased praying for you and asking that you may be filled with the knowledge of His will in all spiritual wisdom and understanding."
–Colossians 1:9

God does not withhold any information that we need regarding His will. But He may not tell us everything. For example, He does not reveal what will happen over the next 10 years. Since He wants us to live in trusting dependence upon Him, He gives us enough light

Remember you have entrusted your life to a loving heavenly Father who plans, promises, and provides only the best. You simply cannot lose when you obey Him.

by which to walk each day. Remember, His Word is a lamp to our feet (Psalm 119:105), not a floodlight to illuminate the highway clear through to our destination. He desires that you and I know and obey His will for us day by day.

As a pastor, I often heard this question: "How can I know the will of God?" People ask this not only when they're trying to determine the overall direction their lives should take but also regarding smaller, daily decisions. Many are confused about whether it is possible to know the Father's will or if He even has a specific plan for their lives.

Be assured: You do not have to fret, because you can completely trust God's will for every circumstance of your life. Although He may not disclose every detail about each situation, His Word provides specific steps you can take each day to learn and fulfill His plan for your life.

When making important decisions, consider the following questions:

- **Is it consistent with God's Word?** Scripture is full of life principles. A single passage can offer wisdom that applies to many situations.

- **Is this a wise decision?** Ask yourself what might be the future consequences of choosing one way over another.

- **Can I honestly ask God to enable me to achieve this?** Remember, anything you acquire outside of the Lord's will sooner or later turns to ashes.

- **Do I have genuine peace about this?** Bring your concern before the Lord. If your conscience and emotions are saying yes and you understand God to be saying yes, then you have perfect peace.
- **Does this fit who I am as a follower of Jesus?** All our actions should be consistent with the fact that we belong to Christ and are to reflect Him to the world.
- **Does this fit God's overall plan for my life?** If the Lord left all choices up to us, then we would be free to make every decision without considering His will. But He has a specific plan for each of His children, and it always is for our best.
- **Will this decision honor God?** Our actions and attitudes should be in keeping with all we know about who God is.

If you are in the process of making a difficult decision and are concerned about the consequences, remember you have entrusted your life to a loving heavenly Father who plans, promises, and provides only the best. You simply cannot lose when you obey Him.

Keep Hope Alive

"I recall this to my mind, therefore I wait. The Lord's acts of mercy indeed do not end, for His compassions do not fail. They are new

every morning; great is Your faithfulness." –Lamentations 3:21-23

Many times, our spiritual insight is limited, but God sees all. He knows exactly what is transpiring on every spiritual level, as well as the entirety of what we are facing. He has a plan, and if we are wise, we will wait for Him to reveal it to us.

Trust and gratitude are powerful forces in the life of a Christian. Believing in the Lord's goodness and being thankful for His faithfulness and provision are indications of our submission to His will, regardless of our hopes or expectations.

Seasons of life may not turn out as anticipated, causing us to struggle. However, because we serve a risen Lord and Savior, no matter what we face in this life, God will bless us as we seek to know Him personally.

Seasons of life may not turn out as anticipated, causing us to struggle. However, because we serve a risen Lord and Savior, no matter what we face in this life, God will bless us as we seek to know Him personally.

Have you trusted the Savior with your unmet needs, or are you still focused on satisfying your hopes and desires your way? Only God can completely meet your needs. Trust Him—give Him your burden to carry—and then wait and watch Him act. And if you have to be patient, always remember that the very act of waiting will strengthen you beyond measure.

chapter seven

Adversity:
He Refines Us by Fire

God Is in Control

"He will ... refine them like gold and silver, so that they may present to the LORD offerings in righteousness." –Malachi 3:3

Cloth can clean the exterior of a piece of gold, but the metal must be refined to remove embedded impurities. That is, it must be melted by fire so that any pollutants can separate and be skimmed from the surface.

The Christian life is frequently compared to this process. When we face struggles, God is refining us like precious metal, digging deep into our lives to eliminate all impurities. He does this not to hurt us but to help us grow into beautiful reflections of His Son.

Too often we hear people exclaim, "Everything is out of control!" Those with little or no belief in an almighty God of the universe find themselves without any source of strength or encouragement when their world begins to collapse. Family heartache, financial problems, or national tragedies–these are all things that

When we face struggles, God is refining us like precious metal, digging deep into our lives to eliminate all impurities. He does this not to hurt us but to help us grow into beautiful reflections of His Son.

we have witnessed firsthand. In the face of such turmoil, how can we be sure God is in control?

If I had to choose a single book in Scripture that powerfully reveals God's complete control from beginning to end, it would be Genesis. In this first book of the Bible, we get to see God working through many different circumstances and obstacles. We see Him as the supreme Lord of creation, making everything from nothing. We see Him conquering sin and death to provide you and me with a way to achieve victory.

Again and again throughout Genesis, we see this pattern: God plans to do something, and despite human unfaithfulness, His perfect will is accomplished. This is the case throughout all of Scripture, and it is still true today. God is in control.

Take Comfort in God's Sovereignty

"The LORD of armies has sworn, saying, 'Certainly, just as I have intended, so it has happened, and just as I have planned so it will stand.'" –Isaiah 14:24

When bad things happen, some people will deny God's existence while others may excuse Him, saying nothing negative is ever His doing. Those who think this way do not understand the Word of God, which clearly teaches God is in complete control over creation.

Let me ask you a question: If God is not in control, who is? If no one or nothing is in control, doesn't everything happen as a result of chance or luck? When Christians throw around the ideas of luck and good fortune, I immediately know they do not fully understand God's Word. Scripture is clear: There are no coincidences with God. He knows what is going to happen at all times. He is sovereign and He is over all things. Everything is subject to His will.

Scripture is clear: There are no coincidences with God. He knows what is going to happen at all times.

When we ascribe things to luck rather than His sovereignty, we're saying there's no plan or order in the universe and we're just victims of our circumstances. God does not want us to live like this. He is in absolute control of every single event in this life. He is the Master over the things that affect His purpose for each of us. When we face times of adversity, instead of minimizing His ability and dominion, we should submit to Him and rejoice in the fact that He is watching over us with love and extreme care.

I remember a particular time when I was struggling with discouragement, doubt, and loneliness. I spent many evenings with a close friend to whom I poured out my heart. Frequently during these talks, my friend stopped me and said, "Remember, God is in control." This statement became an anchor in my life. No matter how hard the winds blew or how much the adversity intensified, my soul remained fixed to the simple truth: God is in control.

God Works All Things for Good

"Behold, the eye of the LORD is on those who fear Him, on those who wait for His faithfulness … Our soul waits for the LORD; He is our help and our shield." –Psalm 33:18, 20

God is in control. His Word underscores this truth, and we can find comfort in the fact that almighty God—who has absolute control of everything—is intimately and continually involved in our individual lives every single day. God never stops providing for, protecting, and caring for each of us. Because He is sovereign and all-knowing, He has perfect knowledge of what we need for today and tomorrow.

And because God is sovereign, we also have the assurance that He will work out every single circumstance in our lives for something good, no matter what. It may be painful, difficult, or seemingly impossible, but God can and will use that situation to achieve His divine purpose. Romans 8:28 makes this clear: "We know that God causes all things to work together for good to those who love God, to those who are called according to His purpose." This statement makes sense only when we realize that He is who He tells us He is— almighty God, infinite in wisdom.

God is our Protector. We have the assurance that nothing can touch us apart from His permissive will. Psalm 34:7 explains, "The angel of the LORD encamps around those who fear Him, and rescues them." When something happens that is painful or unexplainable in our lives, that doesn't mean God has momentarily lost control. On the contrary, we know these things can happen only if He allows them. This hope enables us to go forward by faith, believing that God will deal with every problem or challenge we encounter. He protects us, but He also allows us to face difficulty and even sorrow so that our faith is strengthened.

God is sovereign. No matter what pain, trial, or tragedy comes your way, rejoice that your Father will be there to work it out for your good.

My friend, when you begin to understand that the Lord is in complete control of this world and everything in it, your life will change forever. God is sovereign. No matter what hardship, trial, or tragedy comes your way, rejoice that your Father will be there to work it out for your good.

Tough Training

"Consider it all joy, my brothers and sisters, when you encounter various trials, knowing that the testing of your faith produces endurance. And let endurance have its perfect result, so that you may be perfect and complete, lacking in nothing." –James 1:2-4

Adversity is inescapable, and not one of us is ever happy when it affects us personally. Some Christians say, "Just trust God and think rightly, and you won't have trials." In searching Scripture, however, we see that God has advanced His greatest servants through adversity, not prosperity.

Do you want the kind of faith that is based only on what you have heard or read? It is never your truth until God works it into your life.

God isn't interested in building a generation of fainthearted Christians. Instead, He uses trials to train up stalwart, Spirit-filled witnesses for Jesus Christ. Sometimes, it is hard to hear about the difficulties our friends are facing. But we live in a fallen world and will battle feelings of discouragement. We may wonder, *Lord, what on earth are You doing?*

Hardship is a part of life; it can cause despair, sometimes to the point of disillusionment with Christianity. When we encounter such affliction, we typically say, "It's not fair, God." But we should be asking, "God, what is Your point of view?"

If our lives were free from persecution or trials—if we had everything we wanted and no problems—what would we know about our heavenly Father? Our view of Him would be unscriptural and most likely out of balance. Without adversity, we would never understand who God is or what He is like. How can God prove His faithfulness unless He allows some situations from which He must rescue us? Do you want the kind of faith that is based only on what you have heard or read? It is never your truth until God works it into your life.

Adversity can be a discouragement or God's greatest tool for advancing spiritual growth. Your response makes all the difference. Remember that God has a purpose for the hardship. He's allowed the difficulty, and it fits with His wonderful plan for your life.

God's Presence and Peace

"Cast all your anxiety on him because he cares for you."
–1 Peter 5:7 NIV

We all face stress. The death of a loved one, a tragic accident, or the loss of a close relationship can leave us struggling with feelings of hopelessness, doubt, and confusion. But the Lord has a solution for our tensions and pressures. He knows that we long for peace and safety, and He has promised to provide both for us.

When we cast our burden onto the Lord through prayer, we acknowledge Him as our sufficiency. He is the only one who can adequately carry the weight of a stressful situation.

One of the ways Jesus dealt with the pressures of life was by stepping away from the furious pace of His world to be alone with God. He understood that communion with His Father was essential to maintaining their relationship.

When we go to God in prayer, we express our needs and total dependence on Him. The psalmist wrote, "Cast your burden upon the LORD and He will sustain you; He will never allow the righteous to be shaken" (Psalm 55:22). When we cast our burden onto the Lord through prayer, we acknowledge Him as our sufficiency. He is the only one who can adequately carry the weight of a stressful situation.

Remember that God knows your need for peace even before you ask. And He never grows tired of hearing you pray for His wisdom, guidance, and protection. Don't ever hesitate to take your problems to Him.

chapter eight

Prayer:
Ask, Seek, and Knock

Tenacious Prayer

"Ask, and it will be given to you; seek, and you will find; knock, and it will be opened to you. For everyone who asks receives, and the one who seeks finds, and to the one who knocks it will be opened."
–Matthew 7:7-8

Sometimes well-meaning Christians miss out on fantastic opportunities and blessings because they have taken a completely passive role in their prayer lives. Too often the seeking and knocking described in the above passage are overlooked as a believer merely asks God for something once or twice and then forgets all about the matter.

If you ever hope to defeat your spiritual Enemy, you must begin with active, intentional prayer.

For example, when you begin making college plans, what would happen if you simply sat on the couch and said, "Lord, please show me exactly where You want me to go to college"? Now, on the surface, this seems to be the best way to start the process. But what if you never got off the couch? Suppose that instead of talking with other students, visiting campuses, reviewing school websites and catalogs, and meeting with counselors, you simply sat and waited for an answer from the Lord.

Most likely you would still be sitting there when classes started the next fall!

Or, imagine someone who honestly desires a deeper understanding of Scripture just sets his Bible down on the table and prays, "Lord, please open up the truths of Your Word to me. I desperately want to understand." That person can pray continuously, but without digging into the Word for himself, little will change.

What about matters of spiritual warfare? How should a Christian pray when under attack? Do two-sentence platitudes work then? If you ever hope to defeat your spiritual Enemy, you must begin with active, intentional prayer.

Always Persevere!

"With every prayer and request, pray at all times in the Spirit, and with this in view, be alert with all perseverance and every request for all the saints." –Ephesians 6:18

When you pray, do you have confidence that God will answer, or do you feel unworthy of His attention? Are your prayers specific or general? Is your prayer life a haphazard response to needs and desires, or is it nourishment for the life of Jesus Christ within you?

Prayer is not only asking and receiving but also thanking, adoring, and praising the Lord God. It is a two-way conversation, which includes both divine and human parts—there simply cannot be one without the other. And we are to become actively involved in the process.

Every request, every desire of our hearts, and every need should begin with prayer—bringing our concern to God and seeking to know His will. Because Jesus Christ has come into our lives, we have the privilege and authority to approach the Father through Him and make a request (Ephesians 3:11-12; Hebrews 4:16).

There is a vital element in prayer that most people overlook: steadfastness. We may not see anything happening, but a delay between our asking and our receiving does not mean that God isn't going to answer. He may delay answering a prayer request even if it is in line with His will. Why does He do this? Perhaps He sees wrong motives, bitterness, or unforgiveness—or notices certain unhealthy habits in our lifestyles. God may already have an answer prepared, but He will postpone putting it into action until we are in a spiritual position to

> *Every request, every desire of our hearts, and every need should begin with prayer—bringing our concern to God and seeking to know His will.*

receive it. Or He may be arranging for a number of details to align.

God's timing is perfect. It may not match our own, but you can be sure that it will match His will for our lives. He is far more interested in our knowing Him than in granting our every desire. We cannot grow weary in prayer. When we persist, we gain new insight into the heart of God and reap rewards far greater than some instantly fulfilled request.

Make Prayer a Priority

"Therefore let's approach the throne of grace with confidence, so that we may receive mercy and find grace for help at the time of our need." –Hebrews 4:16

Would you say prayer is a vital part of your daily schedule? There is no way for Jesus Christ to be a part of my life unless I am praying. I talk, share, and relate with Him all day long.

When you go to the Lord, do not be meek and embarrassed; instead, bow before Him and rejoice!

I know Christians who have allowed activities to take up so much space in their lives that prayer is pushed to the periphery. They may diligently serve the Lord, but they are doing this in their own strength and limited wisdom. One of the primary reasons we fail to pray is because we are distracted and don't think we have time to do what is most important.

Why do people do this? I'm convinced it's a matter of denial and avoidance. We deny our need for God. We think that by working overtime, we will gain favor with Him, but all we are doing is draining our lives of His strength.

Nowhere does the Bible say that prayer is easy. It often involves a struggle. There may even be times when Satan will attack you as you pray, harassing you with doubt and sending distracting thoughts into your mind. One of his most effective weapons is discouragement. He wants to tempt you to have feelings of worthlessness. Scripture shatters this plan by boldly proclaiming the truth that you have freedom in Christ to approach the very throne of God in prayer. You are His beloved child—endowed with His goodness and declared not guilty because of His death on the cross. When you go to the Lord, do not be meek and embarrassed; instead, bow before Him and rejoice!

God listens to your requests and wants you to know that nothing is too small or too large for Him. He tells us that when we ask, seek, knock, and trust Him, He will answer and give us His best. This means that many times He will give you what you are requesting. But if He says "no" or "wait," you can be sure that He has something much better in mind.

If you actively apply these simple truths, God will transform your prayer life. Once you establish a prayer time with Him, you will begin to harness His strength to fight your spiritual battles. And when you fight your battles on your knees, you'll win every time!

The Armor of Prayer

"For our struggle is not against flesh and blood, but against the rulers, against the powers, against the world forces of this darkness, against the spiritual forces of wickedness in the heavenly places." –Ephesians 6:12

Have you ever faced circumstances so overwhelming that you wondered how you would stand up under them? More than likely, there will come a time when you have to stand up for what you believe about God. And though you may feel weak, God will give you the strength and the wisdom to speak confidently about your faith. Ask Him to provide the right words to say when others ask about what you believe.

Though none of us enjoy the feeling, vulnerability doesn't have to be a negative experience. If our weakness results in self-pity, despair, or sin, then it is harmful. But if it drives us to depend upon God, it is beneficial. Oftentimes fear and discouragement are caused by the

Devil for the purpose of harming your spirit, soul, or body.

Notice that Scripture does not say, "Arm yourself and go fight the Enemy." Instead, it tells us to stand firm and resist the Devil (Ephesians 6:11; James 4:7). And the only one way to stand is to be firmly planted on the Word of God. So, why does the Bible say this? First, the battle for our salvation already has been won at the cross. Once you are God's child, you are eternally secure (John 10:29-30).

Second, the Lord fights for us. We can do nothing in our own strength. He empowers us to stand firm and advance against the Enemy. Satan, whose goal is to thwart the Lord's plan for us, can do a significant amount of damage. He is out to steal our peace and joy, cause confusion and anger, and encourage wrong relationships. Why? Because he wants to make sure that we are as ineffective as possible.

It is in times of prayer that God teaches us about Himself, His ways, and how we should live our lives.

It is during times of prayer that God teaches us about Himself, His ways, and the way we should live. He releases His energy, divine power, and protection, enabling us to live godly lives—regardless of our circumstances.

Through prayer, our minds and spirits can discern what the average person cannot detect. Prayer is one way God prepares us for Satan's attacks, which may be aimed anywhere—at our finances, relationships, or health. The one thing the Enemy hates above all else is the believer who knows how to persist in prayer and claim the promises of God.

Put on the Armor of God

"Therefore, take up the full armor of God, so that you will be able to resist on the evil day, and having done everything, to stand firm."
–Ephesians 6:13

At all times, we are in the middle of a battle against the powers of spiritual darkness. Satan's goal has not changed over the years. The Enemy knows his ultimate fate, yet he will never give up. The only way he can do damage is by enticing God's beloved children to yield to sin, thus hindering their fellowship with the Lord.

Satan will try to discourage you by filling your mind with doubt and confusion, but you do not have to believe him. The message of the gospel of Christ is given to you as a sure authority.

Paul laid out the battle plan in the sixth chapter of Ephesians. First, we must identify the Enemy (vv. 11-12); second, we are to dress in the full armor of God and stand firm (vv. 13–17). The next verse reveals the key to withstanding Satan's attacks: We must use the strength of the living God. How do we get His power into our lives, to be unleashed in any and every circumstance? There is only one way—by prayer (v. 18).

When you place your faith in Jesus Christ, heaven is on your side.

Whatever transpires in your life, the wisest decision you will ever make is to spend time with the Lord on a regular basis. So make a habit of putting on the armor of God each morning. This is a conscious act of submitting your life to the Lord as your final authority. Acknowledging your need for Him is a sign not of weakness but of unshakable trust. When you place your faith in Jesus Christ, heaven is on your side.

chapter nine

The Bible:
The Instruction Book
for Life

Think Rightly

"What you heard from me, keep as the pattern of sound teaching, with faith and love in Christ Jesus." –2 Timothy 1:13 NIV

What we believe influences our lifestyle and choices. It is the foundation from which we form our opinions and make decisions. For Christians, it is essential to know what we believe and why. Most people inherit their convictions from their parents and simply absorb those ideas without really investigating them.

If our belief system is based upon Scripture, we will recognize deceitful teaching when we hear it and can address real needs with real answers.

To be certain our system of thinking is accurate, we must base it on the Word of God and not on habits, culture, or even family heritage. A belief system is like a safety net through which all outside information must pass. If our safety net has been woven using the truth of the Bible, then we can detect false doctrine and philosophy.

False doctrine is usually mixed up with just enough truth to make it sound good. Many Christians who are not grounded in their faith are easily led astray by doctrines that are genuinely too good to be true. They eagerly support an agenda that is inconsistent with God's Word because it offers license to live according to one's preferences (2 Timothy 4:3).

Believers should know their convictions so they can present those beliefs convincingly to others. While it is the work of the Holy Spirit to bring the lost to Christ, God may choose to use us to instruct unbelievers in the way of truth. Our world is full of people who are desperate, lonely, and hurting. They yearn for the amazing hope that we have.

There is no question that our society is permeated by godless ideas and philosophies that can do great harm. But if our belief system is based upon Scripture, we will recognize deceitful teaching when we hear it and can address real needs with real answers.

Eternal and Timeless Truth

"Sanctify Christ as Lord in your hearts, always being ready to make a defense to everyone who asks you to give an account for the hope that is in you, but with gentleness and respect." –1 Peter 3:15
People often have difficulty expressing what they believe. Instead of having a firm belief system based on godly principles, too many Christians embrace a handful of vague ideas. Peter told us always to be

ready to give a reason for what we believe (1 Peter 3:15), so we want to be sure that we correctly understand Scripture.

Let's consider a list of absolute truths that should be a foundational part of your belief system.

• **The Bible.** In keeping with 2 Timothy 3:16, we refer to Scripture as the inspired Word of God. It is "God-breathed" (NIV), which means the Lord chose individuals to record what He spoke to them. It was given to us so that we might grow in our relationship with Him. This is our instruction book for life and the final authority for what we believe.

> *Peter told us always to be ready to give a reason for what we believe, so we want to be sure that we correctly understand Scripture.*

• **The Godhead.** The truth of the triune God appears throughout the Bible. Our God consists of three distinct persons: God the Father, God the Son, and God the Holy Spirit. They are characterized by the same attributes—they are eternal, omnipotent, omniscient, and immutable—but each person has a different function.

• **Satan.** The Bible tells us that Satan is real. He so desired to be like God that he rebelled against the Creator, who subsequently cast him and his co-conspirators to earth. As the source of all sin, he instigates pain, sorrow, and spiritual death. Christians, however, have no reason for fear, because we are under the protection of the Holy Spirit.

• **Man.** God created man in His image in order to love us and fellowship with us. But when Adam and Eve disobeyed God, mankind's relationship to the Creator changed. At the same time, man's very nature became corrupt so that each of us is born with our will inclined away from God. No man can *earn* God's forgiveness or acceptance. But the Holy Spirit works in the lives of the redeemed to change our nature and turn it back toward God.

• **Salvation.** Salvation is the gift of God's grace, whereby He provides forgiveness for our sins. Jesus Christ died on a cross as a substitute for us. That is, at the time of the Savior's crucifixion, God the Father placed all the sin of mankind upon Him. In that way, our sin debt was paid in full. Now we are sealed in the Holy Spirit and eternally secure.

• **The Church.** The church is the body of Christ, which is made up of believers from every part of the globe. If you have trusted Jesus Christ as your personal Savior, you are in the body of Christ, and God is your heavenly Father. As followers of Jesus, we are to express love for one another—encouraging, helping, and praying for fellow Christians. Our conduct should reflect the heart of our Lord and Master.

Hearing God's Will Clearly

"You will ... pray to Me, and I will listen to you. And you will seek Me and find Me when you search for Me with all your heart. I will let Myself be found by you." —Jeremiah 29:12-14

People use all kinds of methods to make decisions. Far too many Christians choose to say, "Lord, this is what I'm going to do. If this doesn't suit You, just let me know." That is no way to find out what God wants.

God will help you make wise decisions when your motives are pure and you commit to seeking godly discernment.

Having the spiritual discernment to make wise decisions is critical. It is an asset that is not acquired instantly but grows out of a life totally consecrated to and dependent upon God. He will help you make wise decisions when your motives are pure and you commit to seeking godly discernment. He knows your heart and wants you to do the right thing.

In seeking God for perfect guidance, you must first confess your sins and then allow Him to shape your mind and will. When your relationship with Jesus Christ is right, He will give you the wisdom you need.

Are you afraid to make decisions? Do you waver between two paths because you can't determine which way to turn? Perhaps you have a hard time trusting yourself, and you fear the consequences of making the wrong decision. Other times it is sin that blocks your communication with God. How can you know what God wants you to do if there is sin in your heart?

A guilty conscience is to the mind what feedback is to a loudspeaker. When you struggle between your will and God's will, you don't get a clear message. There's nothing but distorted, distracting noise.

Perfect Direction

"The Helper, the Holy Spirit whom the Father will send in My name, He will teach you all things, and remind you of all that I said to you." –John 14:26

Life requires us to make one decision after another. Some are minor decisions and some are major–and many require godly discernment. You may be facing a choice about where to go to college or where to look for work. Maybe you're trying to make a decision about a potential spouse. You're not sure whether it's the Lord's will for you to be married or not. Perhaps you're in college and are trying to choose a major, but you just can't seem to get the Lord's clear direction about it.

Whatever decision you are facing, one thing is certain: God is always willing to show you His will, plan, and purpose. He always desires to give you guidance and direction. God spoke to Abraham, saying, "Go from your country, and from your relatives and from your father's house, to the land which I will

Whatever decision you are facing, one thing is certain: God is always willing to show you His will, plan, and purpose.

show you" (Genesis 12:1). He spoke to Gideon and told him to lead the people of God against those who had enslaved them (Judges 6:14). He sent an angel to Mary to tell her of the Christ child (Luke 1:28-31). When Paul was headed in one direction to preach the gospel, the Holy Spirit made it clear that the apostle was supposed to take a different path (Acts 16:6-7).

God has spoken in many ways, as recorded in both the Old and New Testaments, and He continues to speak to people today. His methods may vary, but the fact that He communicates and gives us direction for our lives does not.

The Word of God is His clear instruction as to how you should live. It is the basis upon which you should make decisions. God has given you Scripture for guidance and training. He also has sent the Holy Spirit to indwell you and interpret the Word so you can have assurance.

God's Guidance in Everything

"I have instructed you in the way of wisdom; I have led you in upright paths. When you walk, your steps will not be hampered; and if you run, you will not stumble." –Proverbs 4:11-12

Have you ever thought about how interested God is in your daily affairs—including those little, seemingly insignificant things that don't make a difference to most people? Christians often separate spiritual matters from the stuff of everyday life, but God never intended for us to make such distinctions.

If you want to make wise decisions, you must live a consecrated life. This means you must surrender your life to the Lord. And it is why Paul said, "Therefore I urge you, brothers and sisters, by the mercies of God, to present your bodies as a living and holy sacrifice, acceptable to God, which is your spiritual service of worship. And do not be conformed to this world, but be transformed by the renewing of your mind, so that you may prove what the will of God is, that which is good and acceptable and perfect" (Romans 12:1-2). If you do this, you can be confident you are walking in God's will. If you persist in prayer, lean on His promises, and wait for His peace, He will speak truth to your heart and mind.

Isaiah 30:21 states, "Your ears will hear a word behind you, saying, 'This is the way, walk in it,' whenever you turn to the right or to the left." This is a beautiful example of how the Lord speaks to our hearts. Day by day, I ask, "Lord, what's next?" And He clearly tells me. The Lord will do the same for you. If you are committed to Jesus Christ—if He is your Savior, your Master, your Lord—and it is your heart's desire to follow Him, you will find a confidence in your spiritual life that you have never known before. If you listen carefully, He will whisper to you very quietly, *My child, this is the way. Walk in it.*

The Pursuit of Wisdom

"Buy the truth and do not sell it—wisdom, instruction and insight as well." –Proverbs 23:23 NIV

The writer of Proverbs reminds us that "The beginning of wisdom is this: Get wisdom. Though it cost all you have, get understanding" (Proverbs 4:7 NIV). So how do we gain the wisdom of God for our lives? We do so when we ...

• **Seek God.** We must believe that if we go to the Lord with even small details, He will hear our prayer and answer it. This is exactly what He does.

• **Learn to meditate on God's Word.** Scripture provides a solution for many decisions facing us. We can trust the Word of God to provide the guidance we need.

• **Learn to obey the principles of Scripture.** Are you willing to surrender to God all that you have so He can live His life through you? This requires not only reading His Word but also meditating on it and putting what you've learned into practice each day.

Human reasoning will fail. Only the wisdom of God will dependably guide you safely through life.

• **Pray consistently.** In times of prayer, we learn to humble our hearts before God. We also learn to be quiet and listen for God's voice through the Holy Spirit.

• **Observe how God works in our world.** At times, the workings of the world may seem out of control. However, always remember that He is sovereign, and pay close attention to the many ways He's orchestrating things in accordance with His perfect plan.

• **Seek wise counsel.** Talk over your problems with trusted Christian friends, a counselor, or a pastor. Then take their counsel to the Lord in prayer.

We seek wisdom to gain God's perspective on our lives and specific situations. Remember that human reasoning will fail. Only the wisdom of God will dependably guide you safely through life.

Lay a Solid Foundation

Yꝏ can lay a strong foundation for your life by accepting God's Son as your Savior and asking Him to come into your heart and forgive your sins. The moment you do this, you are a child of God—a new creation in Christ—and you no longer stand at a distance from the Lord. You belong to Him, and His eternal reward and blessing are yours to enjoy and experience both now and forever.

If you have drifted in your devotion and feel as though you grow more distant each day in your relationship to God, then pray that He would draw you near to Himself. He knows your weaknesses; if you will tell Him you no longer want to oversee your own life, He will come to you in a mighty way and bring hope and light to a challenging situation (Isaiah 55:6-9).

These simple acts are powerful. Tell God that you want your life to be His. Commit your desires, hopes, and dreams to Him, and you will be amazed at the way He works everything together for your good and His glory.

notes

notes

notes

notes

notes